# IGNITE YOUR INNER GENIE

## Your Wish Is Your Command for Kids

Rebecca Anselmo

Book 1

Ignite Success LLC

Boulder City, NV

www.igniteyourinnergenie.com

Ignite Your Inner Genie, Anselmo,Rebecca

Illustrations by Theresa Bower and Adelaida Macias.

Clip art courtesy of   www.clipart.com    Copyright ©2014Jupiterimages corp.

Front cover illustrated by Helen Norsigian Rowles.    helenpainter@cox.net

Edited by Carron Baxter and Stuart Whitehall.

Songs and music by ArleneWow! / Arlene L. Tessman to accompany this book are also available on our website.

Copyright© 2014 by Ignite Success LLC

All right reserved.  No part of this book may be reproduced or utilized in any form or by any means, electronic or mechanical, including photocopying, recording, or by any information storage and retrieval system, without permission in writing from the publisher.

ISBN   9780615903873

Ignite Success LLC

510 Shoshone Way

Boulder City, NV 89005

www.igniteyourinnergenie.com

## Table of Content

| | | |
|---|---|---|
| **Unit 1** | **Your Personal Genie** | **5** |
| | Aladdin's Lamp | 6-9 |
| | Hidden Picture | 10 |
| | Genie's Treasure | 11 |
| | Genie's Home | 12 |
| | You Are the Genie | 13 |
| | Genie Dot to Dot | 14 |
| | Genie's Job | 15 |
| | My Wishes | 16 |
| | Your Jobs | 17 |
| | Our Brain's Job | 18-19 |
| | Your Brain | 20-21 |
| | Creating | 22 |
| | Brain Magic | 23-24 |
| | Bingo Game | 25-27 |
| **Unit 2** | **Who Do You Listen To?** | **29** |
| | Who Do You Let In? | 30 |
| | Who Do You Listen To? | 31 |
| | Choices | 32 |
| | Picture Contest | 33-36 |
| | Who Do You Listen To? | 37-38 |
| | Trust Yourself | 39 |
| | Making Good Decisions | 40 |

|  |  |  |
|---|---|---|
|  | Picture Telephone | 41-43 |
|  | Second Hand News | 44-47 |
|  | Ultimately Yourself | 49 |
|  | Who Do You Listen To? Word Search | 50 |
|  | Colorful Genie | 51 |
|  | Don't Eat Genie | 53-55 |
| Unit 3 | **Teachability Index** | **57** |
|  | Andrew Carnegie Success Secrets | 58-61 |
|  | Learning Puzzle | 62 |
|  | What Did You Learn? | 64 |
|  | Solve the Quote | 65 |
|  | What Do You Think About | 66 |
|  | What Would You Like to Learn? | 67 |
|  | Cup Too Full | 68-70 |
|  | Learning Methods | 71 |
|  | Are You Learning? | 72 |
|  | Enjoy Learning | 73 |
|  | Why Change! | 74-75 |
|  | What Is Poking You | 76-77 |
|  | Time for a New | 78 |
|  | Change Game | 79-80 |
|  | Change It! | 81 |
|  | Mixed Up Quote | 82 |
|  | Teachability Index | 83 |

## Your Personal Genie

**Genie**

treasure

**ideas**

create

**wish**

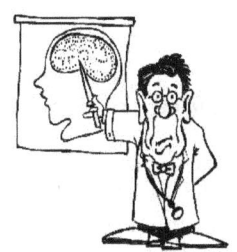

brain

**coins**

lamp

## Aladdin's Lamp

Aladdin is a poor boy.

He could not buy an apple.

He could not buy bread.

He could not buy meat.

One day a man stopped Aladdin at the market.

"Would you like coins to buy apples, bread and meat?" asked the Man.

Aladdin was excited.

"Yes! How do I get the coins?"

"I'll show you a cave that has many coins.

You take the coins.

All I want is the lamp", said the Man.

Aladdin went into the cave.

He saw many coins.

Under the coins he saw the lamp.

Aladdin grabbed the coins and the lamp.

At the opening of the cave Aladdin heard voices.

They were thieves coming to rob the cave.

Aladdin ran back into the cave.

He tripped and fell over the treasure.

A big puff of smoke came from the lamp.

A big Genie bowed at Aladdin.

"What is your wish?" said the Genie.

"You have three wishes.

There are three rules."

One, you cannot change another person.

Two, you cannot change the past.

Three, you can only ask good things for others.

The Genie granted Aladdin his first wish.

"Whoosh!" Aladdin was safely out of the cave.

The Genie granted Aladdin two more wishes.

If you had a Genie,

What would you wish for?

Aladdin's Lamp

Comprehension/ Listening

Color the correct answer

Aladdin was a _____ boy.

happy               poor               rich

Aladdin could not buy _____.

bread               dog                ball

The man promised Aladdin _____.

  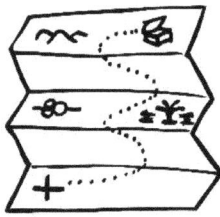  

coins               map                rugs

What did Aladdin find in the cave?

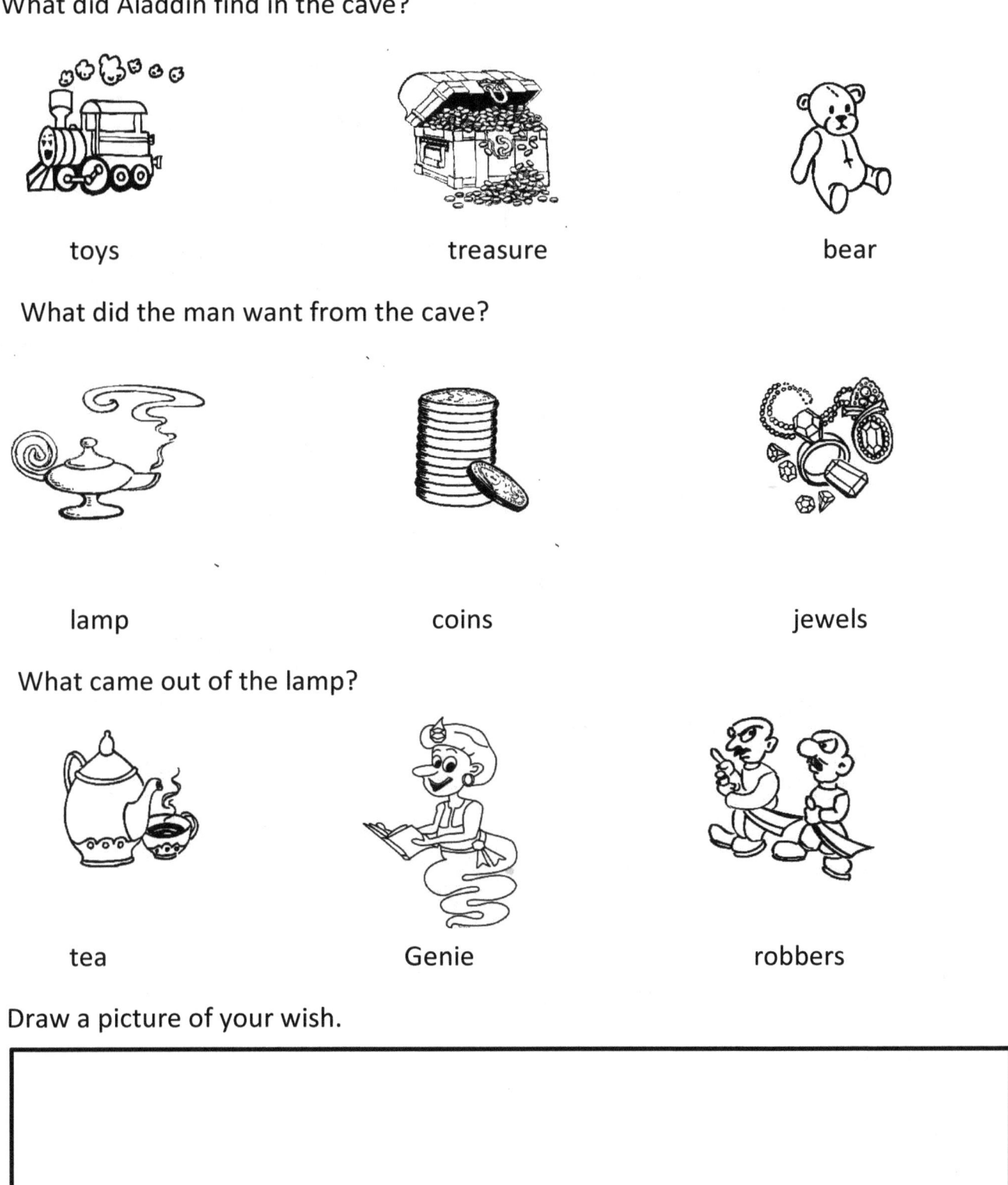

toys    treasure    bear

What did the man want from the cave?

lamp    coins    jewels

What came out of the lamp?

tea    Genie    robbers

Draw a picture of your wish.

## Hidden Picture

Find Aladdin's treasures in the picture.

Aladdin's Treasures:

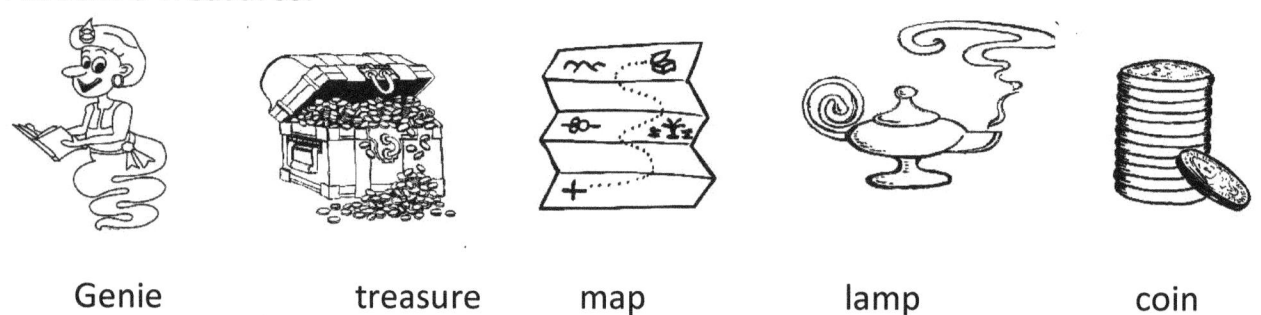

Genie      treasure      map      lamp      coin

Genie's Treasure

The Genie gave you a treasure chest.

What would you put inside?

Draw a picture of what is inside.

Write, what is inside the treasure chest.

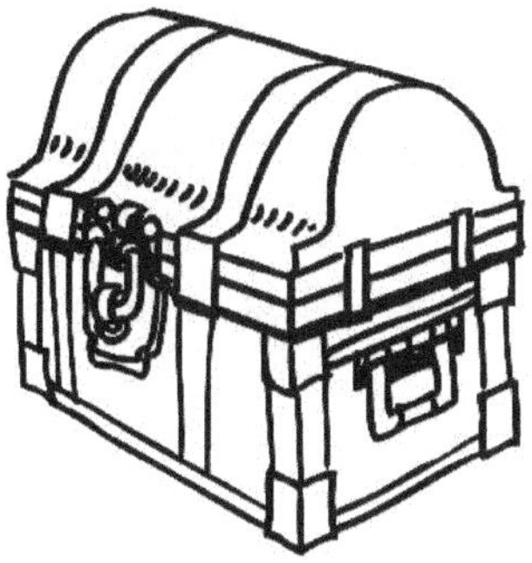

I have _____

_____

_____

_____

inside my treasure chest.

Genie's Home

Aladdin's Genie lives in a lamp.

You also have a Genie.

Where do you think it lives? _____

Solve the code to find out.

How many arms? _____

How many fingers? _____

How many noses? _____

How many toes? _____

Finish the sentence using the code.

The Genie is in your _____

| <u>d</u> | <u>a</u> | <u>h</u> | <u>m</u> | <u>s</u> | <u>v</u> | <u>l</u> | <u>o</u> | <u>c</u> | <u>t</u> | <u>e</u> |
|---|---|---|---|---|---|---|---|---|---|---|
| 0 | 1 | 2 | 3 | 4 | 5 | 6 | 7 | 8 | 9 | 10 |

You Are the Genie

Draw yourself as the Genie.

Genie Dot to Dot

Follow the dots to create a picture of your personal Genie.

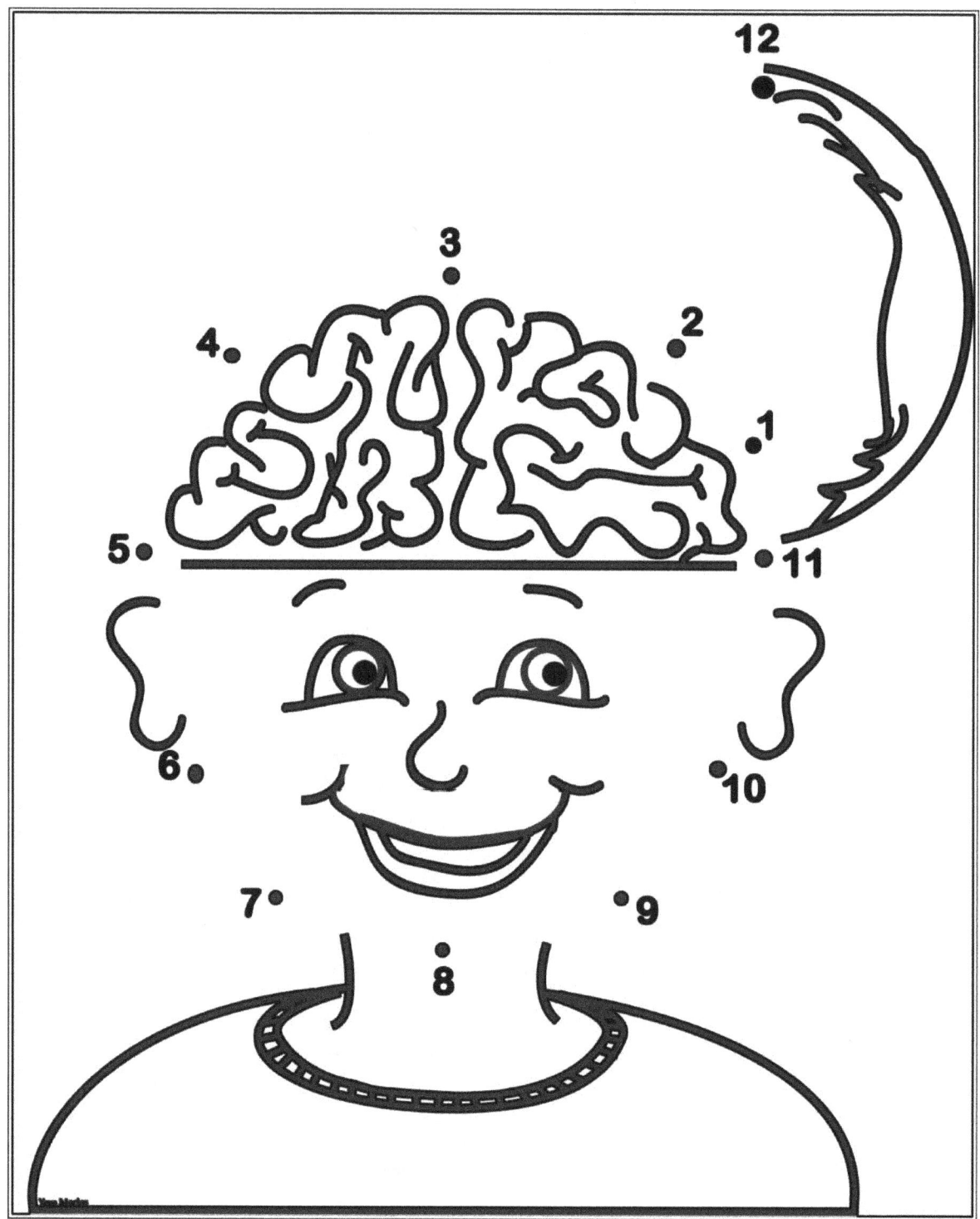

Answer: Your personal Genie is your brain.

Genie's Job

Genie's job is to grant your wishes.

Count how many wishes each kid got.        1  2  3  4  5

_____ wishes

_____ wishes

_____ wishes

_____ wishes

_____ wishes

Do some of these kids have more than 3 wishes?

Yes     no

My Wishes

How many wishes would you like?  _____ wishes

Draw two of your wishes.

## Your Jobs

The Genie's job is to grant our wishes. What are your jobs at home? Color the pictures of your jobs.

dust the furniture

make your bed

water plants

pick up toys

feed a pet

wash dishes

sweep the floor

set the table

## Our Brain's Job

Open the door

Step on in


Your brain is working.

Day and night


It runs your heart.

Whether awake or asleep.


The white blood cells are called upon

Whenever you are sick.


Put your hand on your chest

You are breathing right now


The brains job is never done

There is more for the brain to do.


When you are feeling blue, sad.

Your brain is working there too.

When you jump for joy

The brain is excited too.

You love the taste of that cookie

Your senses show that your brain is working for you.

Write your name

Your brain helps you to form the letters.

Read a book slow or fast

You're receiving a message to move your eyes left to right.

Best of all your brain creates

Like a magical Genie… just wait.

## Your Brain

Color the correct answers.

Your brain is working _____ and _____.

day  night  fish

Your brain runs your _____.

clothes  rabbit  heart

Your brain is working when you feel _____ and _____.

sad  clap  happy

Your brain helps you to _____ and _____ your food.

walk                              taste                              smell

Your brain helps you to form _____ in your name.

letters                           read                              pencil

Draw another way your brain helps you.

Creating

What else does your brain help you create?

Color the pictures of the things you create.

| sandwich | puzzle |
| fish | picture |
| drink | cat |

Draw a picture of something else you create.

Brain Magic

Just like magic your brain makes your dreams come true.

**You can have, be and do anything and everything you want.**

**You can make your dreams come true.**

Draw a dream you want to come true.

## Brain Magic

Draw your dream coming from the hat. Color and hat and your dream.

Bingo Game

One copy for each player or use it as the leader's cards.

| Genie | treasure |
|-------|----------|
| think | create |
| wish | brain |
| coins | lamp |

## Post a Message

Post a message in your bedroom that says:

# I am making my dreams come true.

## Bingo Game

One copy for each player or use as the leader's cards.

| wish | treasure |
|---|---|
| ideas | lamp |
| create | Genie |
| brain | coins |

## Who Do You Listen To?

listen

loving

belittle

don't listen

friends

teacher

family

negative

recognition

positive

**first** hand news

**second** hand news

## Choices

Choose to **listen** to people who are positive, 5-10 on the chart.  **Don't listen** to people who are negative, 0-4 on the chart. Record on the chart for 7 days what you are hearing, positive or negative comments.

| Positive / Negative | Scale |
|---|---|
| I love you! | |
| You are terrific! | 10 |
| You are fabulous | 9 |
| You are a winner! | 8 |
| You can do it! | |
| You are lucky! | 7 |
| All your dreams are coming true. | 6 |
| I like you! | 5 |
| That's too hard! | 4 |
| Why would you do that? | 3 |
| You're not good enough! | |
| You're not smart enough. | 2 |
| Who do you think you are? | 1 |
| | 0 |

## Picture Contest

"Mom the store has a picture contest," said Ann.

"I want to enter."

"The prize is tickets to the zoo," winked Mom.

"What should I draw?"

Ann flapped her arms and spun around, "A bird?"

"The zoo has lots of birds,

Maybe something unusual," said Mom.

"What is unusual?" asked Ann.

"It's something different, like an anteater."

"I don't like anteaters. They aren't cute," frowned Ann.

Ann got home and asked her sister, Kristy.

"What should I draw?"

Kristy cackled spookily, "A Gila monster."

She walked off snickering.

Ann stomped out of the house.

She peered between the slots of the fence.

Her best friend was drawing a picture.

"Amy, what are you doing?"

"I'm drawing a picture for the contest?" said Amy.

Amy held up her picture, "What do you think?"

"It's a beautiful bird," said Ann.

"Are you going to enter the contest?" asked Amy.

"Yeh, I don't know what to make."

"I've got an idea," yelled Ann waving goodbye to Amy. Ann ran to her brother's room.

Zak was drawing on a big canvas.

"What are you making?" blurted out Ann.

"It's a project for art class."

Zak pointed to the canvas, "Imagine, those lines will be a waterfall."

"It's easier to see if you feel it with your heart," he said touching his chest.

"I'm making a picture for a contest at the store.

But I don't know what to make," whined Ann.

"Mom thinks it should be unusual.

Kristy thinks it should be spooky.

Amy has made my favorite bird with lots of beautiful colors.

I don't know what to make now," she gasped.

"Imagine, the feeling you want the picture to have.

"Just by looking at the picture, they will feel your emotions," shared Zak.

"Go ahead! Draw what's in your heart! They will love it!"

Ann drew all afternoon.

Right before dinner Ann dashed over to her Mom.

"Look I finished the picture. It's not unusual, spooky or beautiful. But it makes me feel good."

"Friendship!" said her Mom.

"Two swans that are best friends."

Ann beamed, "You can feel it."

The next week Ann's picture was hanging in the store.

Next to her picture was Amy's with the words WINNER.

Picture Contest

Comprehension/ Listening

Color the picture that answers the questions.

What does Ann want to enter?

running contest          picture contest          bingo contest

What animal did Ann's Mom suggest?

anteater                 rabbit                   dog

What did Amy draw for the contest?

horse                    cat                      bird

Who did Ann listen to?

Brother Zak                    Sister Kristy                    Mother

Did Ann learn from her Mom or her sister?

Yes                            No

Why did she listen to Zak? Is it because he knows how to draw?

Yes                            No

Where did Zak learn how to draw?

art class            cooking class            music class

What did Ann learn? Follow her _____.

  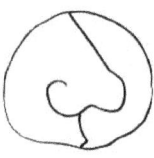

eyes                 feelings                 smell

Ignite Your Inner Genie, Anselmo, Rebecca

## Who Do You Listen To?

People who have what you want.

1. Ann wanted to draw a picture for the contest.
2. Zak could draw.  So, Ann went to Zak for help.

Draw two pictures.

| 1. What you want | 2. Who can help you |
|---|---|
|  |  |

People who came from where you are.

1. Ann needed to learn to draw.
2. Zak was learning to draw.  He was taking an art class.

Draw two pictures

| 3. Is there something fun you are learning right now. | 4. Who can you go to who has learned this already |
|---|---|
|  |  |

Who Do You Listen To?

Draw a line to who can help you.

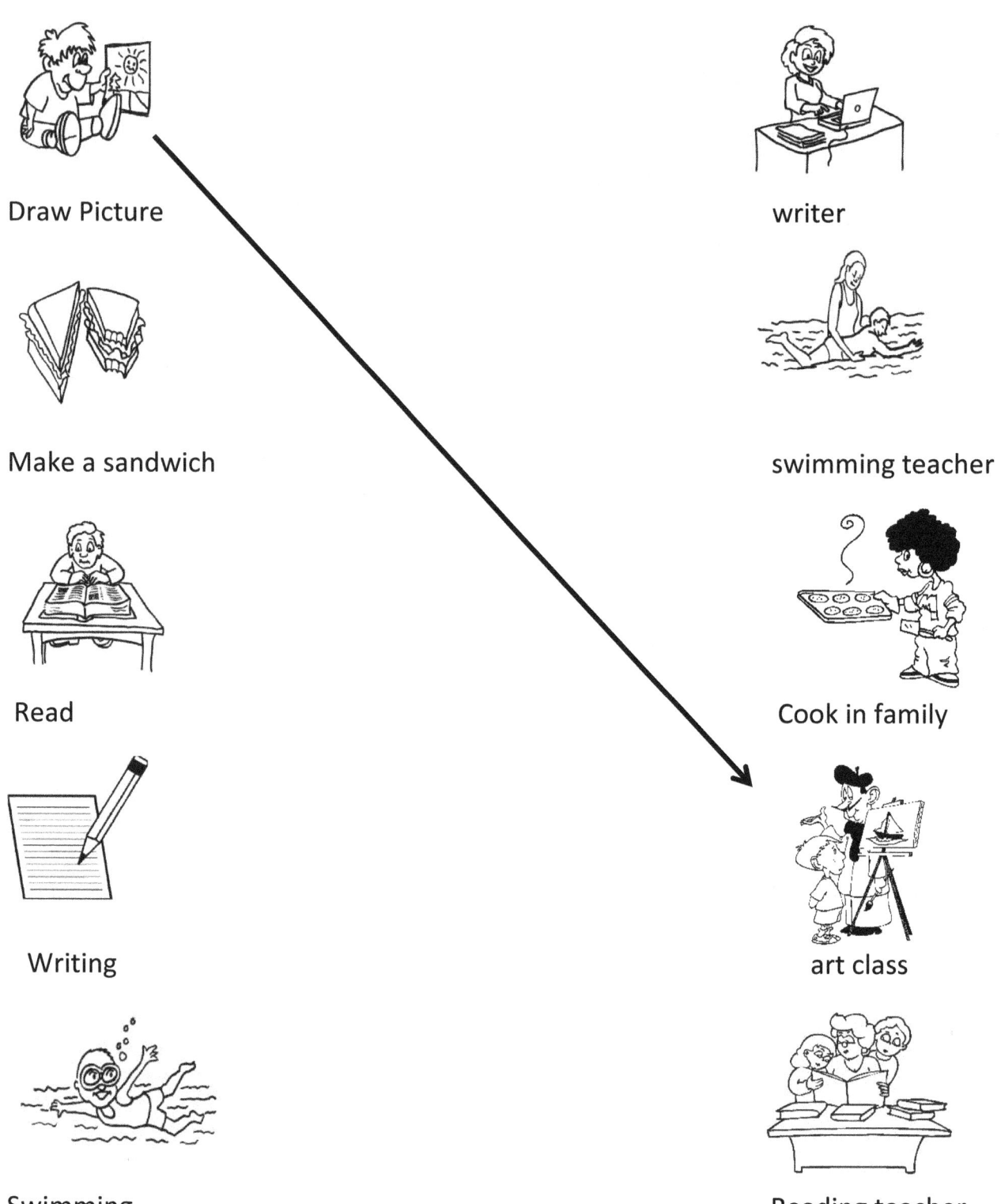

## Trust Yourself

I am good at:

Color the pictures of activities you are good at.

dancing

help others

playing piano

swimming

singing

feeding your pet

math

reading

## Making Good Decisions

Draw a picture of something else you are good at.

Color the answer to the questions.

Are you good at making your own decisions?

Yes            No

Do you pick out your own clothes?

Yes            No

Do you pick a book to read at night?

Yes            No

## Picture Telephone

**Who do you listen to?** You need a group of 3 or more players. Each player gets one picture card. Make up a short story about your picture. One player at a time tells their story about their picture in the ear of the person next to them. Each player then repeats the story into the ear of the person next to them. The last player tells their version of the story to the whole group. Is the story the same when it gets to the last person? Record the answer on the Record Sheet.

Make up your own story

Ignite Your Inner Genie, Anselmo, Rebecca

## Picture Telephone Record Sheet

Did the last person tell the same story as the first person? Color your answer.

1. Story the same?    😊 Yes    ☹ no

2. Story the same?    😊 Yes    ☹ no

3. Story the same?    😊 Yes    ☹ no

4. Story the same?    😊 Yes    ☹ no

5. Story the same?    😊 Yes    ☹ no

6. Your own story    😊 yes    ☹ no

## Second Hand News

Do you listen to second hand news?

 2     "He went to his grandfather's house for a barbeque."

 3     "He went to his Dad's cafe for cake."

4     "He went to his uncle's farm for horseback riding."

5     "He went to his brother's bowling alley with his grandfather."

Where do you think  went? Write the number of the person next to the place they described. Write the number **1** at the place you think  went. The answer is found in the box at the bottom of page 49.

## Second Hand News

## Map

Where are you going to find 🐑 ?

## First Hand News

Always listen to first hand news. If it's second hand news it may be wrong. Cut and paste the information coming from first hand news on side 1 and second hand new on side 2.

| | | |
|---|---|---|
| Uplifting books | Positive CDs | Somebody who has what you want. |
| Someone who has been where you are. | Talking about other people. | Listening to mean comments, you are bad, dumb or lazy. |

## Ultimately Yourself

Ultimately you listen to yourself. Draw a picture of yourself and write what you are going to tell yourself.

| I am terrific. _____ | | I feel great. _____ |

| I am a winner. _____ | | I am lucky. _____ |

| I am a champion. _____ | | I can do it. _____ |

All my dreams are coming true!
_____

If it is to be, it's up to me.
_____

"I'm going to my grandfather's house for a birthday barbeque."

## Who Do You Listen To?

Word search

```
E D N O C E S S K G X U E K P
I Z N K H J D J D O H L V J B
I Q I U Y N Q E X L R O I M A
G X G N E U B J H P F V T M N
L H U I G J X C D H K I I W C
Q T R U T O F Q S L Z N S M X
A F S T E A C H E R I G O B H
K A Q R M D M E V B H S P X J
O V Q I I P Y Q R D D D T V U
E L L U H F L N J V P E I E A
S Y X B K G F N C C K J P S N
P S X Z D G D X W Y W Q B M G
X K J A M F E X F C U K U N K
L J W E S Z X Q Z M Z C S K C
G Z O S G R N C X U H T B B Q
```

FAMILY    FRIENDS    LISTEN
FIRST     LOVING     TEACHER
SECOND    POSITIVE   RECOGNIZE

Colorful Genie

Color the Genie.

## Don't Eat Genie

Place a piece of candy on each picture of the Genie. You will need a team of two to four players. Cut out the cards below. The first player picks a card. If they get the answer the question correct they get to eat a piece of candy. Then they pick another card. If they answer the question correct they eat another piece of candy if they answer incorrect their turn is over. If they pick a card that says **Don't Eat Genie** then their turn is also over. The next player picks a card and the game continues until each person has had a turn.

| Is this someone you want to listen to? I am terrific! | Is this someone you want to listen to? I love me! | Is this someone you want to listen to? You are smart! |
|---|---|---|
| Is this someone you want to listen to? I love you! | Is this someone you want to listen to? I am a champion! | Is this someone you want to listen to? You have what it takes! |
| Is this someone you want to listen to? You are fabulous! | Is this someone you want to listen to? You can't do that! | Is this someone you want to listen to? You're not smart enough! |
| Is this someone you want to listen to? You can do it! | Is this someone you want to listen to? It's too hard! | Is this someone you want to listen to? I'm grateful … |
| Is this someone you want to listen to? I like you! | Is this someone you want to listen to? They don't like you! | **DON'T EAT GENIE** |
| Is this someone you want to listen to? You are lucky! | Is this someone you want to listen to? You're not good enough! | **DON'T EAT GENIE** |
| Is this someone you want to listen to? You are a winner! | Is this someone you want to listen to? You're dumb! | **DON'T EAT GENIE** |
| Is this someone you want to listen to? If it is to be it's up to me! | Is this someone you want to listen to? All your dreams are coming true. | **DON'T EAT GENIE** |
| Is this someone you want to listen to? I can do it! | Is this someone you want to listen to? Who do you think you are? | **DON'T EAT GENIE** |

## DON'T EAT GENIE

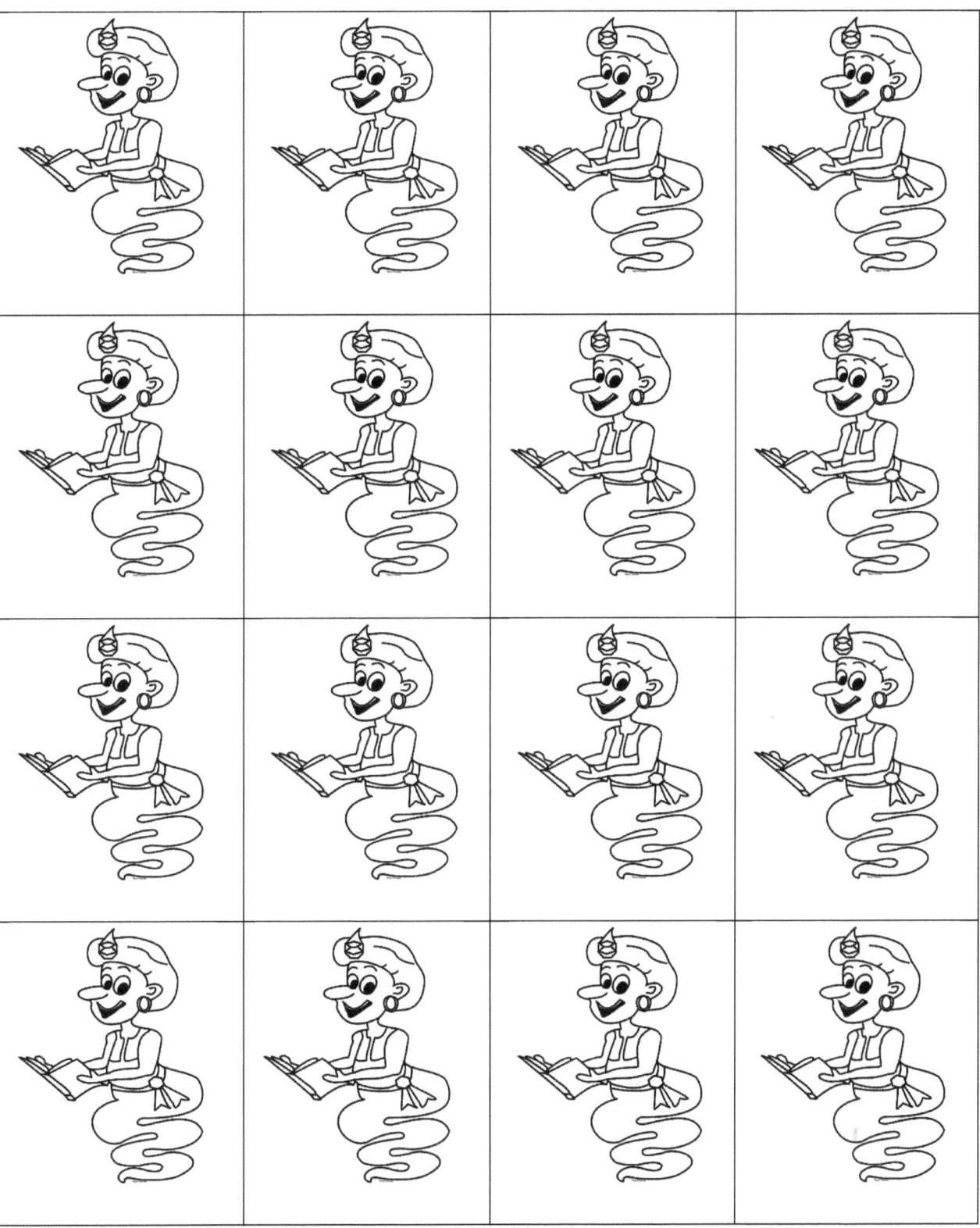

## Teachability Index

| learn | classes |
| --- | --- |
| books | audio |
| change | |
| mentor | easy | experiences |
| relationships | hard |

## Andrew Carnegie Success Secrets

Andrew Carnegie was the richest man in the world in the 19$^{th}$ century.

He was born in a cottage in Scotland.

The cottage had one room that they shared with another family.

Andrew Carnegie's uncle began reading books with him.

In 1848 his family borrowed money to move to America.

They were very poor.

Therefore Andrew got his first job at 12 years of age.

The job was changing spools of thread in a cotton mill.

He worked 12 hours a day, 6 days a week for $1.20.

At age 14, in 1850 Andrew got a job with the telegraph company.

He was paid more, $2.50 per week.

He learned the telegraph signals by ear.

He was so good at his job his boss gave him a better one.

Colonel James Anderson, owner of the telegraph company let the workers check out books from his personal library.

Andrew was there every Saturday to get books.

Andrew Carnegie was a "self-made man".

His willingness to learn and grow brought him many great opportunities.

He became a big success in the steel industry.

This success drove him to help many people.

Andrew gave money to build 3000 public libraries.

He believed anyone could become successful just like him.

His dream carries on today through his love for books and learning.

Ignite Your Inner Genie, Anselmo, Rebecca

## Andrew Carnegie Success Secrets

## Comprehension/ Listening

Color the picture that answers the questions.

Andrew Carnegie was the _____ man in the world.

fastestricheststrongest

Born in a small _____, in Scotland.

cottageapartmenttrailer

His Uncle taught him about _____.

the telegraphbooksmath

Andrew Carnegie and his family moved to _____.

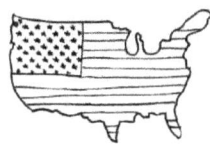  

America                         bigger house                    England

Andrew got his first job at age _____.

10                              11                              12

His starting salary was _____.

$2.50 a week                    $1.20 a day                     $1.20 a week

Andrew worked hard and learned the telegraph signals by _____.

sight                           touch                           hear

Colonel James Anderson lent _____ to his workers.

  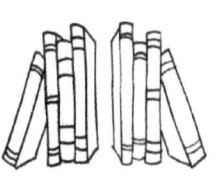

Pencils                         paper                           books

## Learning Puzzle

Cut the puzzle into its pieces. Then complete the puzzle of an object that is an important learning tool. What can you learn? Who can you learn from?

# What tools can you learn from?

The puzzle shows you one.

## What Did You Learn?

Write who taught you how to do each activity.

| What did you learn? | Who did you learn it from? |
|---|---|
| Make your bed | _____ |
| Brush your teeth | _____ |
| Pick up the toys | _____ |
| Make a sandwich | _____ |
| Write your name | _____ |
| Read a book | _____ |
| Play soccer | _____ |
| Ride a bike | _____ |

| Word List | | | |
|---|---|---|---|
| Mom | Sister | Teacher | Classmate |
| Dad | Brother | Friend | adult |

## Solve the Quote

Solve the code and get an important message.   The answer is on page 67.

__Y__ __O__ __U__   __B__ __E__ __C__ __O__ __M__ __E__
25   1   12      14   2   9   1   10   2

__W__ __H__ __A__ __T__   __Y__ __O__ __U__
17   19   4   3      25   1   12

__T__ __H__ __I__ __N__ __K__   __A__ __B__ __O__ __U__ __T__
3   19   13   22   20   4   14   1   12   3

__M__ __O__ __S__ __T__   __O__ __F__   __T__ __H__ __E__
10   1   16   3      1   8      3   19   2

__T__ __I__ __M__ __E__.
3   13   10   2

### Code

| A | B | C | D | E | F | G | H | I | J | K | L | M | N | O | P | Q | R | S |
|---|---|---|---|---|---|---|---|---|---|---|---|---|---|---|---|---|---|---|
| 4 | 14 | 9 | 15 | 2 | 8 | 23 | 19 | 13 | 7 | 20 | 5 | 10 | 22 | 1 | 24 | 18 | 11 | 16 |

| T | U | V | W | X | Y | Z |
|---|---|---|---|---|---|---|
| 3 | 12 | 21 | 17 | 6 | 25 | 17 |

Ignite Your Inner Genie, Anselmo, Rebecca

## What Do You Think About

Andrew Carnegie thought about learning.

He believed in learning.

He learned many things.

| 1835 | 1840 | 1848 | 1850 | 1900 |
|---|---|---|---|---|
| Born in Scotland | His uncle introduced him to books | Moved to America Age 12 | Job at telegraph company Age 14 | Richest man in the world |

Draw a picture or write the things you learned on the time line. (example walking, talking, reading etc.)

Answer: You become what you think about most of the time.

## What Would You Like To Learn?

Color the pictures of the activities you would like to learn.

make money

make friends

good reader

write stories

play ping pong

cook

play soccer

play an instrument

Draw a picture of an activity you would like to learn.

## Cup too Full

Jake was over joyed. He had finally arrived in China.

He spent two years planning and preparing for the trip.

Every day he practiced speaking Chinese.

Read books on how they lived.

Jake enjoyed history most of all.

He spent hours watching movies on Chinese history.

On his walks he listened to audios on China.

Jake was greeted at the door by his Chinese family.

They kindly offered him tea.

Jake chattered non-stop.

"I know everything about China," he said.

"I have been studying Chinese for two years."

Jake continued to talk as they poured the tea.

He shared his knowledge of Chinese way of life.

The Chinese father continued to pour tea into his cup.

Tea began flowing over the rim of the cup onto the table.

Jake, surprised, said, "Why fill it so full."

"You are over flowing with knowledge," said the Chinese father.

"You don't have room to learn more."

Ignite Your Inner Genie, Anselmo, Rebecca

## Cup too Full

## Comprehension/ Listening

Color the answer to the question.

Jake planned a trip to _____.

America          China          England

He read _____ on their way of life.

Books          magazine          newspaper

The Chinese family offered him_____.

Food          tea          cookie

What does chattering mean?

happy          moving          talking

Jake shared his knowledge of Chinese _____.

70

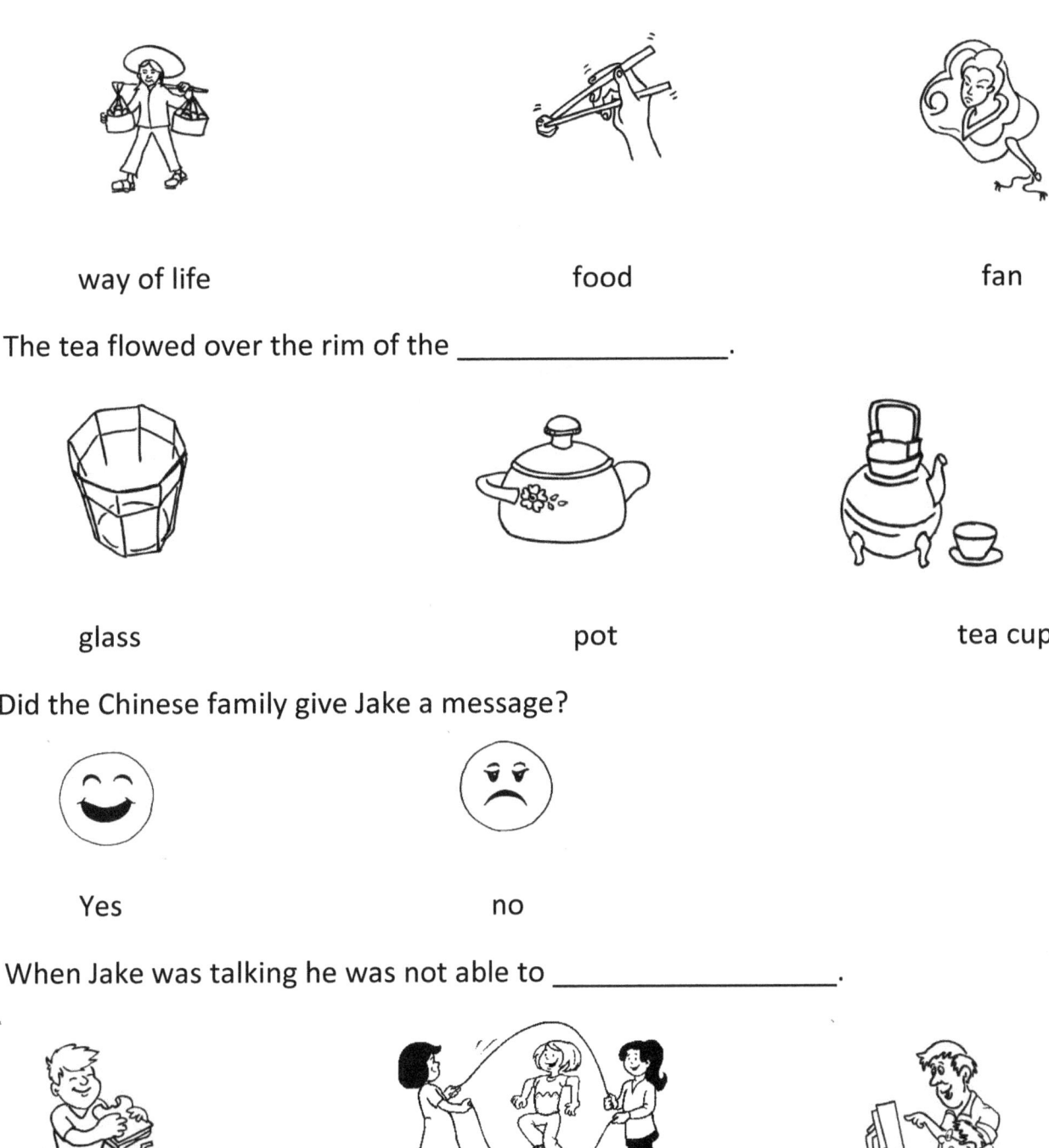

way of life          food          fan

The tea flowed over the rim of the _____.

glass          pot          tea cup

Did the Chinese family give Jake a message?

Yes          no

When Jake was talking he was not able to _____.

eat          play          learn

## Learning Methods

Draw a line to match the pictures of ways you can learn.

books

experiences

audio

class

mentor

relationships

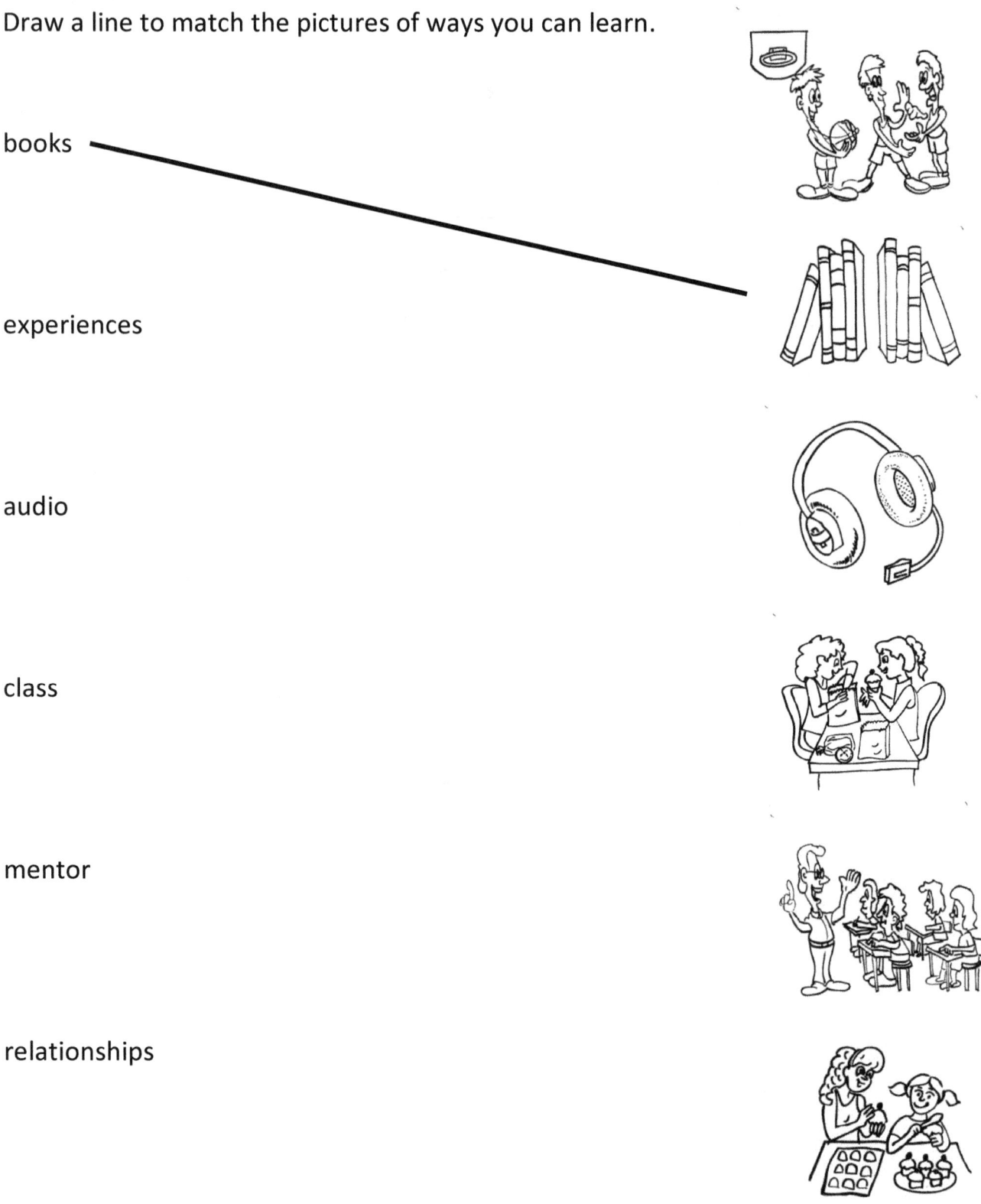

## Are You Learning?

Color the face that answers the question.    yes 😊    no ☹

Are you learning when you're talking?    😊  ☹

Are you learning when you're listening?    😊  ☹

Are you learning when you're happy?    😊  ☹

Are you learning when you're sad?    😊  ☹

Are you learning when you're hungry?    😊  ☹

Are you learning when you're satisfied?    😊  ☹

Are you learning when you're thirsty?    😊  ☹

Do you enjoy learning when someone tells you to?    😊  ☹

## Enjoy Learning

When do you enjoy learning? Draw a picture.

When do you **NOT** enjoy learning? Draw a picture.

## Why Change!

Steve and Robert sat on the front porch. Steven pointed to the dog lying in front of them, "Why is Kane whimpering," Robert said.

"He's lying on a nail poking through the board".

"Why doesn't he just get up and move," Steve grinned.

Robert leaned toward him, "It ain't hurting him that bad yet."

**Color the answer to the following questions.**

Are you ever like Kane, the dog? Not wanting to change or do something different.

yes                                     No

If Kane, the dog likes his spot on the porch, is it easy or hard for him to move?

easy                                    hard

Think about it, if Mom always makes your sandwich for lunch. Is it easy or hard to start making your own sandwich?

easy							hard

Would you change if you were in pain, being poked?

yes							no

The pain of staying still has to be more than the pain of change. Before Kane or you and I decide to move. Pain can be called a POKE. Draw a picture of what you think Kane will do. Will he continue to be poked or will he move?

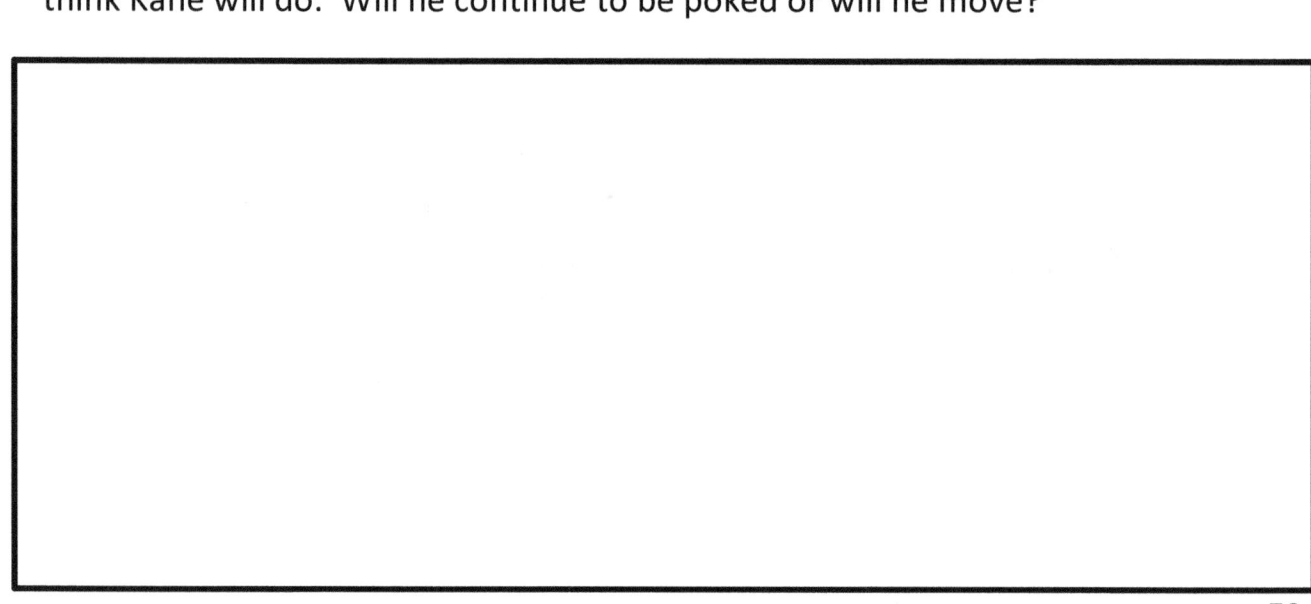

## What Is Poking You

Is there anything that's poking you?   Color the pictures of the things that are poking you.

| Crying | Belittling | Sick |
|---|---|---|
| Lonely | Working hard | Secrets about you |
| Bullying | Hurting yourself | Not understanding |
| Scolded | Broken things | Stealing |

## Poke of Change

Feeling poked is a sign we need to change in one of two ways. Write or draw a picture of each type of change.

1. Our physical body (Kane being poked by the nail. Your pain from tight shoes.)

<br>

2. Our thinking (Pain from harmful thoughts. I can't run fast. I don't know how to do it. I can't get an A on the spelling test.)

Ignite Your Inner Genie, Anselmo, Rebecca

## Time for a New

Is there something poking you?  Do you want to change?

Draw and write about it.

```
┌─────────────────────────────────────────────────────┐
│                                                     │
│                                                     │
│                                                     │
│                                                     │
└─────────────────────────────────────────────────────┘
```

_____
_____
_____


What are you willing to change?  Color your answer     ☺ yes     ☹ no

Are you willing to change your thinking?               ☺         ☹

Are you willing to change your actions?                ☺         ☹

Are you willing to give up things you like?            ☺         ☹

Are you willing to give up feeling comfortable?        ☺         ☹

## Change Game

Direction: Make play dough using one of the following recipes.

### Cooked Play dough

2 teaspoons cream of tartar

1 cup flour

½ cup salt

1 tablespoon oil

1 cup water

Food coloring ( if desired)

Mix the ingredients together in a sauce pan. Cook over low heat until it pulls away from the pan into a big ball. Knead on a board, Color it with food coloring, if desired.

Each person makes a sculpture using the play dough. When the sculptures are complete have everybody in the room rotate clockwise to another person's sculpture. They have 5 minutes to change the other person's sculpture. Then they stand up and go to a new person's sculpture. They continue to rotate until they have changed three different people's sculpture. After the third rotation the players return to their sculpture. Each person completes the Change Game sheet on the next page. Discuss your answers with a partner.

## Change Game

Draw or write how you felt when your sculpture was changed.

Draw or write what you liked about the changes made. What changes would you like to make next time to your sculpture?

Change It!

Change is **good**. Practice changing things so you don't feel

worry      anger      fear    or    controlled, like a puppet

when new happens things happen.

Check off 1 or 2 new things you can change this week.

☐ Change your hair style.

☐ Change the time you brush your teeth.

☐ Change by doing a new job at home.

☐ Change, eat something new today.

Practice changing activities in your life. Whether it's brushing your teeth or reading your bed time book at a different time. Change opens up your eyes and brain to new possibilities.

## Mixed up Quote

The words are mixed up. Put the letters in the correct order to discover a new quote. The answer is found on page 84.

___  ___ ___  ___ ___ ___
f l   u y o   a t w n

___ ___ ___ ___ ___ ___ ___  ___ ___  ___ ___ ___
m t n g i e h s o   n i   r u o y

___ ___ ___  ___ ___  ___ ___ ___ ___ ___  ___ ___ ___
f l i e   o t   e h a g n c   o y u

___ ___ ___  ___ ___  ___ ___ ___ ___ ___
e e n d   t o   n g c a h e

___ ___ ___ ___ ___  ___ ___  ___ ___ ___ ___  ___ ___ ___ ___.
s i t g h n   i n   y r u o   i f l e

Use the words below to complete the quote. Find the words that have been used two times.

| Word List | | | | | |
|---|---|---|---|---|---|
| change | something | your | If | life | in |
| things | need | to | you | want | |

## Teachability Index

Every day for a week keep track of how teachable you are. Write the day of the week on the line that fits your teachability level. A 1 is not teachable all the way up to 10 for very teachable. Do it for 7 days and see if your teachability improves.

10 _____

9 _____

8 _____

7 _____

6 _____

5 _____

4 _____

3 _____

2 _____

1 _____

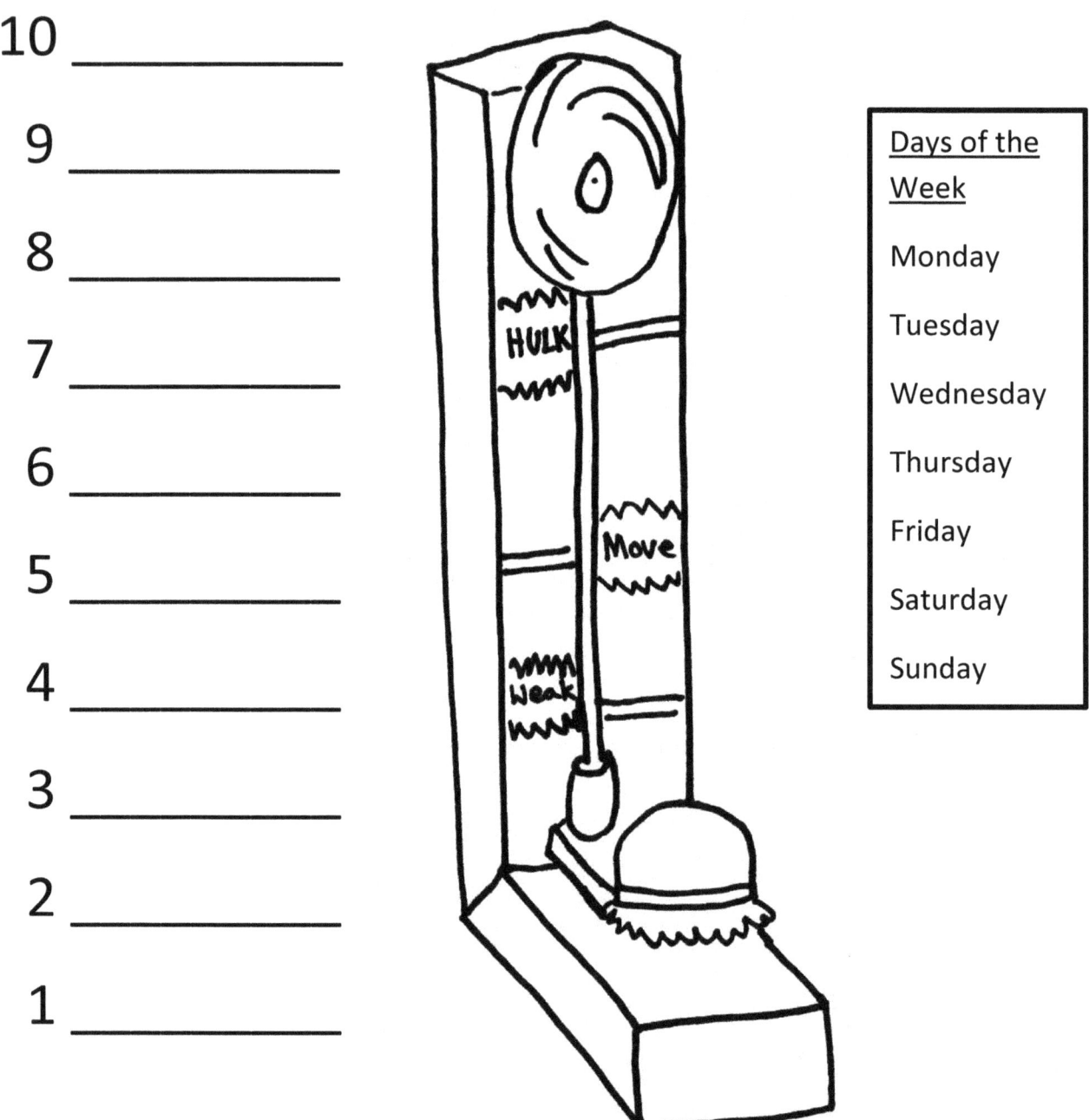

Days of the Week

Monday

Tuesday

Wednesday

Thursday

Friday

Saturday

Sunday

Answer: **Quote** "If you want something in your life to change you need to change things in your life."

# Additional Products

## Ignite Your Inner Genie Series

**IGNITE YOUR INNER GENIE**

**BOOK 1**

Introduce your child to their personal genie. The interactive activities in this book will show them the first two steps in activating this incredible gift.

**IGNITE YOUR INNER GENIE**

**BOOK 2**

Accelerate your child's ability to reach their potential for success through these engaging activities. Steps 4, 5, and 6 shows the child how to master their inner genie by applying it in school or a home.

**IGNITE YOUR INNER GENIE**

**BOOK 3**

Good food is important for a healthy body and your child's inner genie. Help your child explore what it takes to nourish that genie. Engage in activities that strengthen and expand this inner knowledge to reveal hidden secrets of creating their dreams.

Order at: www.igniteyourinnergenie.com

**IGNITE YOUR INNER GENIE**

**CD**

Dance and sing with these catchy tunes that bring joy and delight to any home or classroom. Each song reinforces the concepts taught in IGNITE YOUR INNER GENIE books 1-3. Let your child activate their inner genie today.

**TIPS FOR PARENTS
CULTIVATING A STRONG
PARENT-SCHOOL RELATIONSHIP**

Parents engage in
meaningful partnership
with their child's school

**TIPS FOR TEACHERS
IGNITE PARENT INVOLVEMENT**

This booklet reveals methods
to engage parents in meaningful partnership
with their educational institution.

Order at: www.igniteyourinnergenie.com

A Magical Adventure Poster-

This poster reminds you to believe in the

Magic of your dreams.

Magical Moments Poster

Create your own magic using this poster

to transform any situation into something

positive, magical.

www.ingramcontent.com/pod-product-compliance
Lightning Source LLC
Chambersburg PA
CBHW081500040426
42446CB00016B/3330